Shattered Starlight

SUHANI GOYAL

To all those who found themselves here despite it all

Contents

Desire Mirrored

A girl dimmed by shadows dark as night
Insignificant, unwanted, unremarkable
The list of what she is and what she'll never be
As eternal as the unlit night itself
The same night she remains eclipsed by

That's what the mirror, revulsed, displays
Yet it's not what the girl herself sees
She finds solace in the allure of the stars
She finds comfort in the beauty of the moon
Yet a small, insignificant part of her remains
That yearns for the seraphic light of the sun

A girl bathed in swaths of silk, pure as light
Hair like flowing water; shifting, cascading
Beautifully ethereal as the day, smile so bright
She's the kind preserved forever behind glass
Glass that can only wish to be so delicate as her

That's what the mirror, awestruck, displays
Yet it's not what the girl herself sees
She views her light as blinding, smile as duplicitous
She knows of how others crave what she has
Yet a significant part of her still remains
That yearns for the simplicity of starlight

And so the sun chases the moon relentlessly
As relentless as the moon, who chases the sun
They are all but cat and mouse, trapped
All but the minute hand and hour hand of a clock
Cursed, forever; to meet only once in a blue moon

One wishes desperately for dazzling beauty
The other wishes for modesty- clarity
Others know nothing of their curse
For each desires what the other has
Unbeknownst that each looks at the other
With that same desire mirrored

Reflections by The Neighbourhood

Runaway by Aurora

Wanderlust

People always talk, and talk, and talk
Of this place they so blissfully call 'home'
Of a place so warm, sunlit, solacing
They return, always, no matter where they roam

Yet this word they speak of so fondly
This word they spend lifetimes searching for
It is a word spoken in a foreign tongue
For a 'home,' for me, is nothing but lore

Roaming with no care for finding it
Is all but a myth; something simply unheard of
To live life without a so-called 'home'
But is to be without a home truly to be unloved?

For I have no home; no home has me
Yet even nowhere, home is everywhere
For I find freedom fleeing from these confines
By the trap of four walls, I shall not be ensnared

I allow myself to do what only fools wouldn't;
I allow myself to get lost so as to be found
To experience the wonder in wanderlust
For when you could fly, why stay on the ground?

'Home' may seem to be a feeling unfamiliar
Yet for me that is all that it is- a feeling
For a house is not a home
A set of four walls are not the key to healing

Losing your mind thinking of losing home
What's truly foreign to me is that fear
For how could you lose what was never there
Yet still always was, and has been here

Unsent Letters

Those letters we left unsent
Those words we left unspoken
Those tales we left untold
Those wishes we left unsaid

They take the form of regret
They take the form of remorse
Of sleepless nights and wondering
Just constantly wondering 'what if?'

What if I had sent those letters?
What if I'd said those words?
What if I'd dared to wish upon a star?
Would that have changed our ending?

Regret is the one and only
That upstages even doubt
For it is regret that stays
Even as doubt takes its leave

Each choice changed our story
Everything unspoken was our undoing
And only those fallen stars know the depth
Of my longing for a different end

But fate has had her way
And you shall never cease to exist
As long as I have with me
My unspoken words and unsent letters

Cinnamon girl by Lana Del Rey

This is me trying by Taylor Swift

Weighted Inadequacy

Disappointment
A funny word, is it not?
Of course, you would know
It's all you've ever felt

I was never enough for you
I was a burden; a chore on your list
A curse in the distant past, distant future
Never what you wanted from me

You can ridicule me
You can make me feel weighted inadequacy
You can make me lose everything
Every last shred of pride I've felt in myself

Endless nights, I've *killed* myself
Ruined myself in hopes it'd be enough
But nothing I've done or could do
Ever has been or will be enough

Disappointment, a figure familiar
It's wraps around me
A figure lurking in the darkness
Fed by your relentlessness

I am so, so tired
So tired of your escapades
Tired of treading so carefully near you
When all you'd ever do is let me drown

A pit lies where your heart should be
You go around, entitled,
Shattering people like glass shards, useless
But are they glass or are they mirror?

Are you disappointed in me?
Or are you just scared I'll be better than you were?
Because I can be inadequate, if you want
But I'll never let myself be what you've become

Meadow Moonlit

A last wish upon a fallen star
A clandestine meeting
In a meadow moonlit
Moments forever fleeting

The keeper of all our secrets
That lakeside glade
We lay facing the waterfall
Watching the water cascade

The low calls of the nightingale
The hyacinth's sweet perfume
Surrounded by trees evergreen
The meadow's beauty consumes

Away from the grays of the city
The city we both fled from
Our moonlit meadow offers solace
To the desire of freedom we succumb

We remain together forevermore
As long as that meadow remains
That beautiful, moonlit meadow
Where serenity forever reigns

Somewhere only we know by Keane

We fell in love in October by girl in red

Castles Crumbling

Streets, lined with vibrant shops
Deserted in the pouring rain
The wind whispers sweet nothings
Thriving in serenity's reign

A palace in the distant hills
Shrouded in ivy vines
Captivating despite disrepair
Within its own world, enshrined

The smell of earth and rain mingle
Intertwined with the aroma of coffee
Heaven on earth; my safe place
The silence echoes ever so softly

Is it really so strange?
So strange that I've found comfort
So strange that I bask in the autumn chill
The melancholic tones, to me, dulcet

The deepest of browns to the coolest grays
Leaving me mesmerized; enchanted
The beauty of emptiness incomparable
A seed of wonder, in my heart, planted

Familiarity wraps around me
As I walk these hallowed streets
All but a novel to accompany me
To clear my path, everyone else retreats

How violently soft the leaves fall
The castle in the distance crumbling
A thin layer of frost blankets my safe place
Into a world of fantasy, I'm tumbling

The Fallen Rose

The roses I gave to you
Lay in a glass vase, vibrant
The sun shone brighter,
The stars aligned,
Clouds became ever so light,
Time itself stilled to watch.
It was fate, it was destiny,
You meeting me.
But time is a cruel, cruel being.
He takes away everything,
Everyone.
Again. And again. And again,
Until he leaves you with nothing,
Nothing but a vault of emotion undesired.
Nothing but the unwanted memory
Of your last words, whispered
In a dark room barren of joy
Whispered to me like loss on a breeze
You said to me the only thing
The only thing that stopped me
From following you into the darkness
'If you lose something,
It's never really lost,' you told me
And so lies the hope in my heart
The hope of meeting you
In another world; another lifetime
As the roses I gave to you
Lie at your grave, wilting

The exit by Conan Gray

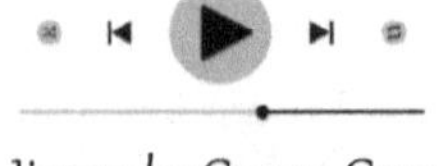

Jigsaw by Conan Gray

The Facade of Hope

When you trust people repeatedly
Let pure hope fill your heart
Let it blind you each time
Every time, inevitably
The trusted tear that hope to shreds
And as the facade of hope vanishes
Despair smacks you in the face
Clarity makes its grand entrance

The cycle repeats
Again.
Again.
Until you can trust no more
Until you guard your heart so well
That heartless you shall seem
You lock all feelings and blazing emotion
Behind a sealed, impenetrable vault

And all that's left of the person that was
Is a hollow, lifeless husk
Spirit broken, trust betrayed
The shell of the person that was
Tethered to the earth
But only just barely
But only temporarily

Stolen Glances, Stolen Heart

With stolen glances, you stole my heart
With unspoken words you spoke my truth
With secrets told, and secrets kept
You took pieces of me one by one
And I gave them to you all too willingly
Never knowing you'd have taken them anyway

I should've run from you
But that was always your thing, wasn't it?
How many times did you have to leave
For me to learn to leave you in the past?
They say that time heals, and they were right
Time heals; but people never do

The world of words that you left unsaid
Take up unwanted space in my mind
The world of hurt that you left at my doorstep
Still there, waiting, till this day
Because all too much reminds me of you
When all I want is to forget

Love was all but a fire, burning bright
And while everyone else ran for safety
I let myself fall into the depths of the flame
Thinking I would find you waiting for me
But you left me with nothing but memories
Memories I wish you took with you
When you took the broken remains of me

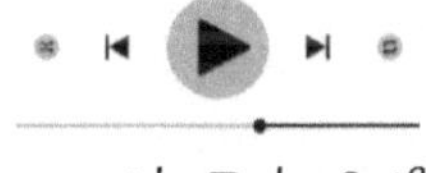

august by Taylor Swift

Panic room by Au/Ra

Panic Eternal

That feeling felt as often as change
That sinking weight, low in your gut
That feeling that's so incomparable
That feeling that's so inexplicably electric

There are no words to describe it
That sinking, electric feeling
However, ironically enough
It can be described by a simple word

Panic.

Knowing that it may be your last time
Your last time with that one person
Your last time walking those familiar halls
So many lasts all at once, overwhelming

More weighted than the lasts are the firsts
Your first time saying goodbye
No matter how many times you feel it
The firsts are forever a constant

Eternal.

The end is not the end, it is the beginning
At least, that's what they say
However, they who speak are those
Who simply wish that panic away

To say goodbye is no little thing
Yet when you do it as often as breathing
Then the pain and the panic fade away
And slowly fade away the scars from leaving

The Ocean's Whisper

On a small isle in my memory
A small strip of land
In the middle of nowhere
I first experienced true beauty

The salt, the clarity in the air
The whispers of the ocean
As it reached out to shore
Its love for the sand requited

The pure turquoise waters
Clear and all knowing
The sunset skies so effervescent
Laughs loved and lost to the wind

I could've sworn the sun smiled
The isle itself glowing with it
And nothing, absolutely nothing
Could compare to it

That feeling I'd never experienced
Some beautiful, evanescent mix
Of pure bliss and ecstasy
Etched in every part of me

Even in that moment, however
On a small isle in my memory
A small strip of land
In the middle of nowhere

I experienced something familiar
For it was sorrow and despair I felt
Knowing that nothing, absolutely
Nothing could ever compare

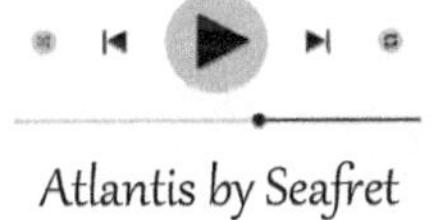

Atlantis by Seafret

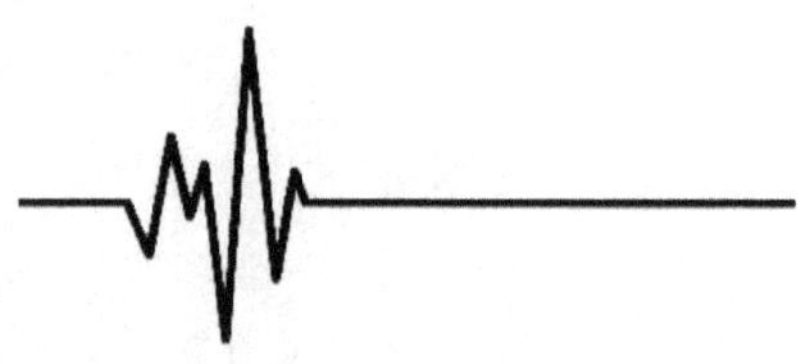

I wanna be yours by Arctic Monkeys

The Rhythm of the Heart

It's as scintillating as the sun
As purely blissful as the day
It's fingers glide along my skin
Like a warm breeze in May

It offers silent companionship
In the darkness of night
Free of the judgment of people
It offers some solacing respite

Each note is a whisper in my ear
As evanescent as emotion
It pervades each and every sense
Not unlike the water of the ocean

The rhythm of the music
Beats in time with my heart
The melody flows effortlessly
A breathtaking work of art

The dulcet tones are a constant
There even when they're not
Present forever in heart and mind
Reality is a faraway thought

For when music plays, gone is reality
Gone is the uninvited presence of life
All that's left is me myself and I
And that? That is when I truly feel alive

Paper, Ink, Letters Merge

Snowflakes perform intricate dances
A pure white veil envelops the earth
Glistening frost adorns every window
The epitome of serenity and mirth

I lounge in a plush, cushioned chair
A fleece blanket draped around me
My cup of coffee emanates warmth
From reality, I contentedly flee

For there remains no room for reality
When extraordinary worlds await
Retained within a riveting book
My interest shall never abate

Within the infinite ocean of fiction
I've been hopelessly, irrevocably submerged
Tethered by imagination and ingenuity
Paper, ink, and letters merge

Breathtaking as the real world can be
Nothing compares to the world of books
Guilty pleasures, we all tend to have
But here is mine, reading in my little nook

Sweater weather by The Neighbourhood

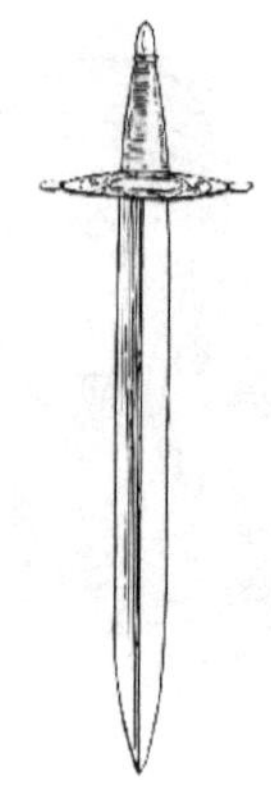

War of hearts by Ruelle

Love and War

"All's fair in love and war."
The phrase I hate most
Because in what world
Was what you did to me fair?
I chose love
But you declared war
The person who was supposed
To love me the most
Was the person who wished
Hoped and prayed for my ruination
Was the person that caused it
Because that's all you know to do
All that you've been taught
An endless generational cycle
Of violence, and trauma, and war

Repeat.

And so I wilt, letting my petals fall
Like a rose left to die
On a desolate battlefield
It's '*my* fault,'
You're so fond of saying
I was the one who caused our end
That's how you like to tell our story
With you playing the victim
And me the eternal villain
But aren't villains made, not born?
You are the one who ruined me
So I ruined you in return
Now you can shed as many tears
As many tears as it takes
To fill the river you dried up
But I won't say a word
I will not apologize for healing
Because isn't all fair in love and war?

Underwater

The feeling of being underwater
So surreal, it's indescribable
The feeling of being submerged
So unthinkably calming

The silence underneath
From above the surface to below
Something found only in the deep
Something so deeply underappreciated

The water flowing around you
Moving despite being still
The feeling of being completely
And utterly alone, yet never lonely

Time stands still with you
A friend rather than foe
But to find time's friendship
You must let yourself sink

The feeling of sinking
Never as pleasant
Weighted pressure holding you
Holding you back from emerging

No, it is indeed unpleasant
Yet a reality that has to be faced
For you have to let yourself sink
Before you can ever swim

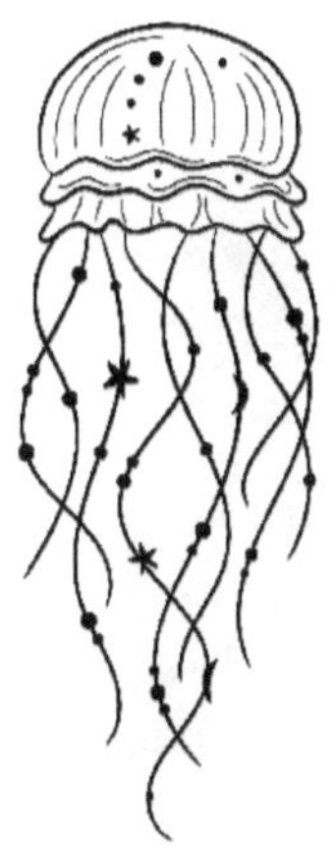

Summertime sadness by Lana Del Rey

Block me out by Gracie Abrams

Glass Shards

For some people, I am transparent
Yet even transparency has layers
Layers of deceit, of ego,
Of hopelessly unspoken words
All layered into something so fragile
Something so fractured
The facade splinters with one fall
To reveal something deep
A pit of glass, eternal
Something so deeply unending
They say I am transparent
Yet if I am transparent,
What, pray tell, are they?
Everyone has layers
And everyone will someday break
For we are all but shards
Of a broken mirror
But shards hurt; shards cut
Every word they speak
Is a shard of them given to me
A shard designed to cut

Loss and Starry Nights

If you offered her the stars, she'd refuse
Because she hates them for taking him from her.
If you offered her the ocean, she'd refuse
Because it'd remind her of the tears she shed for him.
If you offered her a pair of wings, she'd refuse
Because no wings could ever take her to him.
If you offered her the sun or the moon, she'd refuse
Because neither are as bright as he was.
If you offered her the world, she'd refuse
Because it's worthless without him in it.
She doesn't want the ocean, stars, sun or moon.
She doesn't want the world.
She just wants him back.

Dancing with your ghost by Sasha Alex Sloan

Je te laisserai des mots by Patrick Watson

A Museum's Embrace

Each museum of art holds within it
The flickering flame of an artist unlit
Without language, their words spoken
And still their spell remains unbroken

Each painting is a sight to behold
Each stroke tells a story untold
A thousand secrets concealed
Secrets, only to the stars, revealed

Each person, each life, fated one day to fade
Each castle to fall at the mercy of a blade
Yet one thing remains forever timeless;
Their portraits in a museum, priceless

From days and friends lost to time
From words forgotten to forgotten rhyme
Forgotten is not, a museum lost
It, in itself, soothingly accosts

From every sunset to each night sky
From palaces of Vienna to Versailles
Every corner of every place
Art is found, like a warm embrace

From every memory of coffee eyes
To blazing bonfires on moonlit nights
Captured by a single work of art
Enshrined eternally in the heart

Losing my Mind

Their screams echo in my head
Whispers. Screams. Or are they mine?
I've lost time, numb to all feeling
With the feeling of loss, losing my mind

The intensity with which the clarity appears
Is overwhelming and yet familiar
I'm losing it again, I whisper to myself
In the light, my tears are almost silver

Sometimes, all alone, I can admit
Without fear, doubt, an ounce of restraint
It's their fault. Every moment of numbness
With their words, it's my mind that they taint

With their stares speaking just as much
I search for escape; but people don't come with an exit
How did I get here? Burning, burning, burning
Perhaps because within me, a roaring flame they have lit

And so I turn to ashes beneath them
Peace is one of those unknown creatures
Like the ones that lurk in my mind
Each a face brimming with *their* features

Each one, just another part of me
A gift yet a curse from no one but them
Because this is a pain only *they* can inflict
They are the ones you should condemn

Not me
Not me
Not me

For I am not the one who made me
This thing that you despise so much

Family line by Conan Gray

Experience by Ludovico Einaudi

Crimson Echoes

Her laughs echo,
her pure white dress
flowing behind her
as she sprints
across the meadow
in the mountains
adorned with flowers
as vibrant as her
he watches her, stricken
heart near bursting with joy
his face coloured by wonder
and awe at her beauty
she remains unblemished
by the cruelty of the world
unblemished by truth
years later, here she stands
in the same scenic meadow
her screams echoing
in the expanse of the mountains
dressed in a deep crimson
as dark as blood
she screams at the world
until her voice breaks
screams until she's as raw
as raw on the outside
as she is within
knowing that no one
no one can hear her
but in the depths, he can
her every scream
recklessly tears him apart
until he can stand
the agony no longer
her every scream hurts him
more than comprehensible
as he remembers those days
before the world scarred her
the days when she could laugh

Falling Timelessly

The autumn leaves fall
Just like me, like you, like us
They fall endlessly

But I'm done falling
Falling hopelessly with you
Falling just for you

I'm so done giving
Giving, yet never getting
So I give you up

I watch as you leave
As you leave without regret
Void of emotion

All that's left of you
A moment frozen in time
An icy heart, timeless

Autumn to winter
My foolish heart stops longing
With the seasons' change

Tolerate it by Taylor Swift

Ophelia by The Lumineers

Season's Change

She's a bliss
A warm breeze
Sunlight on skin
Sand and ocean
A bonfire at the beach
'Tis a bright melody
That lies in her laugh
She is the sound
Of warmth and joy
Wild and free
A vivid summer day

She's a bliss
Snowflakes ever-
graceful
And ice that glistens
Under the starlit night
Frost that whispers
Carried by a gentle
zephyr
A warm cup of coffee
A fire at the hearth
Beauty in her silence
Allure in her beauty
A tranquil winter night

She's a bliss
Petals scattered
Flowers at her feet
Lush, verdant valleys
Crystalline streams
The sun emerges
With a bird's song
A vibrant light
Lives within her
'Tis the bringer of life
The dawn of spring

She's a bliss
Leaves dancing
To the beat of rainfall
The sun at eventide
Hues abundant
Cinnamon spice
And amber eyes
Clandestine meetings
The mark of change
Solace and comfort
Idyllic autumn evenings

Acknowledgements

A huge round of applause to everyone that made this book possible.

Firstly, to my parents, who not only inspired some of these works, but also helped throughout the publishing process.

To all my beta readers, especially Mehar, without whom this book would've remained a first draft void of meaning.

I would also like to thank all those who listened through my 3 AM poetic rants and made sure I wasn't going crazy throughout the writing process (you know who you are).

Last but not the least, to all those who are holding this book right now; this collection was a dream made possible thanks to each and every one of you.

Signing off!

Suhani

www.ingramcontent.com/pod-product-compliance
Lightning Source LLC
Chambersburg PA
CBHW021143130726
47988CB00003B/1448